GOLDMINING
the
SHADOWS

PIXIE LIGHTHORSE

Lighthorse Publishing, 2019
Redmond, OR

GOLDMINING
the
SHADOWS

HONORING THE MEDICINE OF WOUNDS

"You are the antidote you have been longing for. This book guides you in unearthing this truth. This book will help you become medicine to the earth. This book is the work we are desperately needing in the times we are living. I cannot think of a better guide or chaperone for this necessary and invaluable work. Let the gentle and wise hand of Pixie, lead you through the dark to your well of light."

– Sarah Blondin, author, *Heart Minded*

"Pixie cracks the door open to the shadowy places that exist within our hearts, and then allows us to walk through it with her steady hand as our guide. A beautiful, thoughtful read for the world today."

–Missy Rhysing, Ritualcravt

"Part road map, part manual, I stood up from my seat a completely different person after reading, much to my fiercely protective shadow's chagrin. Pixie writes that 'soul work flourishes in safe company' and auspiciously provides an unquestionably safe place to begin so that we can stop harming ourselves and others with our woundedness."

–Anne Carmack, Writer & Artist

"This book speaks directly to the soul and says 'here you go, this is the work you've been waiting to do. This accessible way in is going to make the collective work all the more possible."

— Amanda Stuermer, World Muse Founder

"It may be the most important work in our soul's evolution and healing, to walk with courage and clarity the shadow landscapes of our souls. This book serves as a velvety manual guiding us into and through the intimate intricacies of these dark places. Pixie offers both guidance into the depths, as well as tools and the support of a clear container, which can lead us to alchemize the shadows into gold, thus bringing us into growth and greater wholeness."

—Marysia Miernowska, Author, *Witch's Herbal Apothecary*

"Pixie's ability to shine a loving light on shadow work is a gift. She's skilled at gently guiding the reader, while also encouraging personal accountability. Goldmining the Shadows *is a powerful resource for anyone wanting to fully embrace a more open-hearted life and relationship.*"

—Julie Jeske, MS, LPC, Sex and Relationship Counselor

AUTHOR'S NOTE

I began writing *Goldmining the Shadows* while stumbling through a conversation about the concept and value of hope. I was in favor of it then, because I know how terrible hopelessness feels. During the writing of this book, my view on hope has changed.

While hope is "the thing with feathers" according to Emily Dickinson, I have come to think of it as a numbing medication. Hope, for many of us, provides a too-instant sigh of relief. Even if I occasionally find it helpful, I know that my job is to know the truth and be with it. While I may be growing a few feathers, my job is to keep walking and do the thing in front of me.

Hope's shadow is fear, ignorance, and oblivion. There are aspects of modern life fueled by fear, ignorance, and oblivion. We have not evolved to be able to manage our existential anxiety yet. It physically wears us down. We are, however, together in our avoidance, and that is comforting. The Amazon rainforest is still burning, after months of clear-cutting and mismanagement by those voracious for short-term gain. The lungs of the earth have received precious little care for these long-term consequences for all people. I can't help but feel hopeless and fearful at times. The thing to do is what we can do—become strong with bandwidth to face how things actually are, not yearn for how we want them to be. This is bioremediation. The more pollution we can break down, the more we can introduce healthier options. I like to start within, where prior conditioning is polluting our intelligence, sound judgment, and our relationships to each other on small and large scales.

There is no part of my vocation that requires me to be hopeful or give hope. I've held that in my pocket as a reminder to honor transparency. I wrote this book to enliven, uplift, and strengthen you to keep walking. Grab the hand next to you as you go and share an impassioned glance of knowing. Let understanding be your fuel and mine, not hope. Let's stop trying to fly away on a few unsteady feathers and instead deepen our love and willingness to be with ourselves, one another, and what is. Let our ability to walk together generate the sigh of relief we really need.

Pixie Lighthorse
September 2019

To the wounded but brave
who are making their way through the labyrinth

and

Willie Laverne, the guardian of my spirit

FOREWORD

Tending, befriending, and integrating shadow is the great work of our times. We have our hands full in this particular historical moment. We are living under a huge, unchecked collective shadow—one that covers the globe.

For many decades I've been a Shadowlands guide. My first journey with my shadow almost killed me, because I was entranced by the darkness and what I found. Early in my addiction recovery, I went back into this realm like a hotheaded gunslinger—intending to kill all that had once entrapped me. Really, I was shaking in my boots, afraid that what I encountered would swallow me whole.

Instead, I met the biggest surprise of my young life: the first glimmers of real freedom. Gradually, as I repeatedly returned to the Shadowlands, I recovered my sovereign self, owned my power, and inhabited my own skin. I came to trust that no matter what was discovered or revealed, I had the presence and tools to live with it and transform. I discovered the essence of me within my shadow, the gifts of lineage, and parts of my soul.

Shadow has become a buzzword meaning "everything bad about you." This is not so. Although your entry point to real shadow work may be looking at your "character flaws," or areas where you need to grow, the nitty-gritty work of shadow is unearthing and discovering what is nonconscious. The moment we look in the mirror, we begin the work of moving toward the most important peace talks there are—those between our divided parts and our warring parts. If we can't hold this, we surely will not create changes in the groups and communities around us.

The fugitive self, our hidden gold, the things that won't let us rest, our traditions and lineages—cobwebbed and musty—are in some cases booby-trapped to prevent extraction and exploitation. The point is to heal our lineages and be capable of reparations, both big and small, individual and collective. Learning to hold the pain and contradictions of our own shadow, wrestle and be with them, is how we ripen. This seasoning eventually becomes wisdom.

You were born to do this work. You are made for this. Pixie has evoked the essence of a wise guide to travel with you into your Shadowlands. This book wants to be worked with, written in, cried on, talked back to, and stained with experience. It is a guide to distill the medicine hidden in the raw ingredients of wounds and fragmented stories.

Pixie embodies the strength of kindness as she calls us all to go beyond earnest self-improvement into the heavyweight work of becoming who we truly are—capable and contributing to healing this beautiful world that we all have the privilege of inhabiting.

Shannon Thompson
Founder, Shakti Rising

CONTENTS

INTRODUCTION

Pain is something we can all relate to. We have grown socially accustomed to looking for a magic pill to mask it. Becoming intimate with pain, but not possessed by it, enables us to feel, sense, and hear the wise teachings held within it. Individual and collective pain, as well as pain carried for Earth during this time of great transition and liberation, contains valuable wisdom.

What value exists in exploring the textured landscape of our wounds?

Shadow is a term for the discarded aspects of our personalities within that inform our lives. It offers the potential to reveal what we previously thought was unsuitable, so unsuitable that we imprisoned it and forgot it. The aim of healing is to know the shadow well, appreciate it and seek to integrate it—not leave it neglected to rot in a cell beneath the surface, resigned to clanging its tin cup against the bars asking for acknowledgment and honoring. Your shadow is worthy as part of your life story, but it is not useful as the operating manual.

This is not a book that pits light against dark or suggests you get to know your darkness to achieve mastery over it. Its aim is to help you access and honor the qualities in you that went underground, adapting to help you stay safe. Its purpose is to prime you for ongoing dialogue with your subterranean influences, which were born from experience, generational trauma, and family conditioning.

The process of understanding your shadow may seem studded with landmines—a precarious endeavor that will make it more difficult to manage ordinary daily life. It could sound the alarm on familial relationships limping along on old resentments and grudges. It may ask you to take too much responsibility and make uncomfortable changes. Burrowing through the pains of your life promises no immediate or transcendent peace, so why go there?

You can opt to leave the curtains drawn and find ways to medicate what still hurts.

You can deny and protect, in order to save your self-image or shield others who have hurt you.

You can conserve energy by not seeking to fix what isn't visibly broken.

Or you can dig. You can go willingly into it. You can unearth what lies beneath the tip of your iceberg, and free yourself from the nonconscious influence of your ancient sufferings.

You may feel that it's time to be honest with yourself—to be transparent about what shaped you. You may want to know more about shelved hurts that caused you to adapt for protection and emotional survival.

What drives the need to contend with what we've been through? Is it our desire for deeper intimacy and connectedness? To be seen, known, and loved despite our bruises? Maybe we dig to develop self-compassion, knowing that once we come to peace with ourselves, we can offer empathy to others. These bodies we walk around in are conditioned for self-loathing. Most of us are addicted to the belief that we are inadequate—it keeps us striving to be better, and isn't that a good thing?

What will it take to feel connected, secure, and enjoy a sense of belonging? Healing is becoming a high priority, and marketing enthusiasts are onto us. Our hunger for wellness supports a 4.2 trillion dollar industry, according to a 2018 study conducted by Fast Company, and shows no signs of slowing. Many remedies only scratch the surface, offering topical solutions for conditions of the soul that no coach, workout or pill can fix.

The point of doing shadow work is to grow strong enough to endure emotional pain while making adjustments that will help achieve the desired outcome. Many engage the mishandlings of the past on the therapist's sofa, hoping for at least short periods of internal peace, and more harmony in relationships. Others look desperately for a greater sense of security. We seem to be one big, dysfunctional global family, growing closer together in proximity and further apart emotionally.

Exploring the origins of emotional patterns brings conscious awareness to difficult moments of interaction. Behaviors motivated by fear and insecurity show up as "fight, flight, or freeze" responses. Our autonomic nervous systems send our bodies and brains clues all day long about what feels intense, but most often, we ignore them. Behind our moments of struggle to cope with daily stress and relationship triggers are legions of little untended wounds closed up tight in a trunk in the basement. At some point, we are called to sit on the dusty floor to sift and sort. It is a voluntary process that requires some time, and possibly a giant box of tissues.

Think of a time when you recently flew, fought, or froze. What was it like to feel a rise in your internal meters and be on edgy alert? Your internal first responders are a compass pointing you toward the medicine embedded in the pain you're still feeling.

Tuning into the body's signals—sweaty palms, belly aches, increased heart rate, fear, anger, rage, nervous tendencies, obsessions/fixations, addictive cravings—helps us to be aware so we can liberate ourselves from obstacles that stand in the way of peace, serenity, calmness, strength, and resilience. Strengthening our relationship to the force holding us captive is what helps us wiggle free from its bonds.

What is shadow?

Swiss psychoanalyst Carl Jung coined the term "the shadow" in the 1940s. Today it is thought of as the psyche's reservoir for what we find unacceptable about ourselves. This "shadow" is made up of many parts, mostly hurts from very early in our lives, from our parents, caregivers, adopted and/or foster parents, and those who came before them.

What do shadows do?

The nonconscious shadow wreaks havoc on our lives. It is what we are referring to when we speak about slaying our dragons and battling with our demons—these are interior fights with a force that can feel like it's trying to do us and those around us serious harm, and the results are reflected in how we treat and are treated by others. A nonconscious shadow holds us hostage, victimizes us, or causes us to seek control through domination. We each contain all of the weapons of violence imaginable, right inside of us. This can be a frightening thought, yet it promises to re-empower us to grow beyond harming ourselves and others. This is the pivot-point where healing begins. Compression eventually seeks to elongate. It is time to breathe space into the tightest places and create fluidity.

Imprisoned by our nonconsciousness, the dominant culture and early memories that informed our path, our shadows are frightened inner children afraid of rejection and recrimination. Because the shadow is forsaken by the protective ego, isn't attentive of its presence. It's a driving force within us, but we aren't aware of it. We are instead weaponizing our hurts against ourselves and others scapegoating what we can't face in ourselves. In its way, the shadow is seeking to get even for what is still out of balance going all the way back to our developmental years. For colonized nations, we must go back to the birth of the systems that used oppression to be successful.

Shadow can be thought of as our psychological dungeon, containing many restless inhabitants: the forgotten, disowned, subterranean parts of ourselves that reside quietly inside of us waiting for an opportunity to come to our defense. It can be challenging to grasp when we don't know it exists and therefore don't know how to work with it to heal.

How do I work with my shadow?

The key to working with your shadow is to accept that you have one, and get to know it. See it for what it is and nurture it as your child while you build adult techniques for self-protection.

Peeking voluntarily behind the curtain of what formed your adulthood is a courageous move. To engage in shadow work when you aren't triggered helps you get ahead of it and direct traffic. Gazing into the murkier parts of your family's origins and underlying generational patterns yields valuable awareness about all of the moving parts and influences that have shaped you. Doing this with intention is a very big deal. With practice and some support, you can move beyond feeling victimized and into a more powerful stance. It's a super-heroic task if you consider that heroes always have tragic flaws that keep them humble and in service to others.

We begin grooming our shadows for the future by experiencing the shadows of our caregivers: adapting to their habits, adjusting for their needs, harmonizing or rebelling against what is imbalanced in the models they offer us. We also imprint features from the culture in which we develop: taking on unwanted/forced roles and responsibilities, observing taboos and acceptable practices, and aspiring to be more like those celebrated by the collective. We learn how to be by looking at other people all around us and making exterior choices to help us feel more secure. How you respected your emotions determined what you needed to stash internally to be acceptable. You can probably name the emotions that were not okay to have when you were growing. This is a great place to start shadow work.

Healing your shadow means partnering with it in order to understand it better. Sometimes our real-time life partners are the ones that trigger us, poking sharply on the places we need to heal. Our primary relationships can become places to become more well when significant others and/or close family members prioritize healing and can offer empathy to each other. The mirror of a partner can provide an accelerated path when wellness is a relational priority.

Shadow work is an act of liberation for individuals and all members of society and culture. Once we have a grasp on what our personal shadows are and how they work, we can empathetically address the collective shadow that has our communities and societies in its grip. It is entirely possible to reshape our collective reality by catching our shadows in the act of responding to historical pain. Our repetitive loops of suffering cause ripples of stress and stress-related disorders in the body. Doing shadow work is one of many keys to breaking the cycles that contribute to ill health.

When we make space for understanding shadow's influence at the household level, we open up the possibility of insight into what is happening in the greater world. This is healing, both internally and externally.

In writing this book, I confronted my shadow many times. Though I've been in dialogue with my interior territory for the last twenty years, it still shows up when I risk meaningful expression. I overcame its concerns by taking breaks, examining my fears, and reassuring it.

If you've found yourself reading this book, perhaps it is because you are looking for the treasure in your depths. To support the work of inner excavation, you must stop denying that your shadow persistently tries to have its way with you. You have the choice to be enriched by what you find, or to seek the familiar shelter of past coping mechanisms. Autonomy relies on your willingness to spin the straw of your wounds into gold for a more whole and treasured life.

My wish is that *Goldmining* will be a supportive voice in a constellation of resources for interacting with your wounds. It is intended to connect you to your deep personal wisdom. My desire is for this work to reveal the beauty that you came into this world with before you adapted for your family, the culture, and the times. I hold the vision that you can love your soul profoundly, despite all it has had to do to survive here. I'm rooting for you, while still wandering the bogs learning to love and value the medicinal distillations of my own agonies.

HOW TO USE THIS BOOK

Goldmining the Shadows is meant to help you honor your healing. You may have to say no to other priorities for a little while. It takes time, energy, and personal space to support yourself in a process of growing beyond your current skin. Attending your healing offers the treasure of intimate experience and self-understanding. In a decade of creating healing spaces, I have yet to hear anyone say that they wish they hadn't made time for their healing.

It's my experience that the shadow doesn't stop coming up and rearing its ugly head. It's here to stay, because it was formed by your early examples of what adulthood looked like. What you don't have to do is take direction from it. The goal is to see clearly what it's doing to your relationships and progress beyond the usual internal and relational dramas.

I invite you to move through this book at your own pace, and be there for yourself through what challenges you. Bookmark pages that bring up feelings and discomforts.

Goldmining is written in bite-sized nuggets so you can balance your inner work with periods of "rest and digest"—clinical shorthand for what the nervous system does when it's in a parasympathetic state (not reacting with fight-flight-freeze).

Set yourself up for success by making a declaration for your healing process:

- I'm taking care of myself.

- This is how I'm courageously engaging what is true for me.

- I'm looking at old narratives and seeking to transform them.

- I'm hurting in ways I can't even put my finger on.

- I will likely need support from truly available sources.

- My unhealed wounds are affecting me and my loved ones.

- My unidentified wounds are impacting how my life is turning out.

- My culture's wounds are hurting me and others—I want to change that.

- It's worth my emotional resources to know more about what's eating at me.

- I want to be clear on what I haven't made peace with.

- I and many others will benefit from my healing process.

- I am willing to look at some hard truths to grow and do better.

- My shadow work contributes to culture repair.

What does shadow work offer me?

- Liberation
- Departure from codependency
- Relief
- Autonomy
- Sovereignty
- Maturity
- Empathy
- Compassion
- Humility
- Security
- Elevated perspective
- Trigger management
- Coping skills
- Self-understanding
- Healthier relationships
- Greater belonging and connection

What's this book prompting me to do?

This book asks you to take responsibility for the parts of yourself you are most driven to deny—to be accountable to your blind spots. They are the influences most negatively impacting your life and the world you live in. When we acknowledge our power to cause great pain and suffering, we reduce self-harm and harm to others. Collectively, our habits harm the earth and many people daily.

Your individual healing is a healing for the collective. One hazard of an untended shadow is that it leaks out onto loved ones, into society, our communities, into our politics, and the environment. Our shadows have had a large part in shaping the world we live in, and what we most often seek to change about it.

This book will be useful to you if you value healing and are willing to break through toxic, repetitive patterns that lead to diminished and destroyed relationships, to yourself and others. It will serve you well if you have a genuine desire to be a beneficial organism on the planet, guided by empathy and your willing heart.

GLOSSARY OF TERMS

Ancestral wound: an inherited chain of addiction, violence, or other limiting belief system.

Angst: a feeling of deep anxiety or dread, typically an unfocused one about the human condition or the state of the world in general.

Bioremediation: clean-up of pollution by introducing new organic material.

Catharsis: productive release of stored emotions.

Ego strength: humility to hear feedback, admit mistakes, and move forward with repairs.

Invulnerability: the condition of being impossible to harm or damage.

Narcissism: a personality disorder caused by severe parental neglect resulting in reflexive self-centeredness.

Nonconscious: not consciously aware of.

Personality disorder: a type of mental disorder featuring rigid and unhealthy patterns of thinking, functioning, and behaving.

Projection: a defense mechanism in which one's own perspective is projected onto another.

Psyche: the human soul, mind, and/or spirit.

Reparations: the making of amends and compensations for
                         wrongs and injuries.

Resilience: the ability to bounce back after a big challenge
                         or overcome an ordeal.

Shadow: a weak or inferior remnant or version of an
                         individual, community, or nation.

Victim: a person harmed, injured, or killed as a result
                         of a crime, accident, or other event or action.

Vulnerability: exposure to the possibility of harm.

GOLDMINING
the
SHADOWS

PIXIE LIGHTHORSE

MAKE A NEST

Before beginning to unearth your shadow, identify ways to create space that are favorable for depth-level soul work. The environment around you may be full of daily to-dos and interpersonal matters so be sure to check in with your inner landscape.

Working with breath, sleep, and diet can help create a foundation conducive to emotional healing inside of you. When undertaking healing, it's easy to overlook these three basic life functions. Our body systems need extra support when healing because we spend large quantities of emotional energy processing for understanding. Composting fear and pain in order to grow self-compassion and overall wellness is alchemy, which needs fuel and functionality. It may take a year of venting and grieving to process your subconscious contents. Decisions can wait. It is not wise to make major life changes while you are engaged in shadow work.

Like a mother preparing for birth and fussing over the nursery, prepare for the inward trek to retrieve truth. You'll be digging through memories held in the shoeboxes of your mind, so formalize the occasion.

Prepare to nourish yourself. Schedule check-ins with friends and appointments with counselors, have books on hand about your types of trauma and conditions, and set aside time to reflect. We live in a time where resources for healing are plentiful. While some cost money, many do not.

Deciding to face, once and for all, the contents of shadow can be a bit like taking on a part-time job. Tending to ourselves requires space, time and a gentle bedside manner.

HUNT LIKE A CAT

Feline, feminine, carnivorous, luxuriously attentive to self: cats are the ultimate teachers of self-care. In my previous book, *Boundaries & Protection*, mountain lion paces a golden, protective circle around the reader to bring awareness to the energy of personal space. For shadow work, panther demonstrates fearsomeness and the lessons of woundings as nourishing medicine.

Cats clean and groom themselves unceasingly, serving as a reminder to clean our internal and external spaces of hang-ups and worn-out beliefs about ourselves.

Big cats are apex predators, known for preying on small rodents and game and keeping the environment in balance. Think of panther as your guide for understanding and knowing how to be with your shadow. Panther is a nocturnal and crepuscular animal that hunts stealthily at dusk, dawn, and through the night in the thick of dense rainforests and jungles. Think of your shadow reactions as the scurrying creatures that panther stalks, whose subtle presences are overrunning your internal processes with habits no longer useful to you and that do not serve your well-being.

If you have ever observed a cat, you have likely noticed that they sense things that humans do not perceive. They have a propensity for picking up on slight movements, which is the key to their ability to hunt efficiently and stay full.

When you utilize your intuition and sensory perception to detect what is crawling around the inner landscape of your mind during quiet times, you are apt to find what you are seeking.

HOW SHADOWS ARE MADE

Your shadow got its start when someone else's ideas of how you should be were imposed on you. When you were asked or forced to conform to structures that harmed you, and you didn't have the power to protest, adaptations became beliefs about who you really were.

When you began to individuate, you may have been considered selfish. What you felt ashamed about, you pushed down. This may have benefitted the people who didn't like your behavior, but it didn't help you. Negative beliefs about who you were began to alter your growth and development.

It may never have become safe to talk about what you hid to protect yourself. Your hurt feelings may not have become known to your family, and so they could not help you reverse the beliefs. Insecure caregivers are not usually open to feedback about what it felt like for you to be harmed or neglected by their words, actions, and inactions. Some caregivers are not present at all, and their absence is a source of pain that compounds as time goes on. Some harms were not intentional, while others were. Some were inflicted "for your own good," which sent a confusing message to your developing system.

The shadow includes contents known and unknown about your inner being. Some shadows may be formed by all that was not allowed to be in early childhood, or that was deemed wrong or unsuitable by caregivers, parents, or peers. You expertly created a version of yourself that you thought would eventually get you the love and care you needed most in exchange.

SHADOW'S SPECIALITIES

Your shadow specializes in protecting your most fragile parts. It works as it was designed: to keep you from being seen as you do not wish to be seen and to avoid further injury, embarrassment, and pain. Anger or toughness may have been assets in your family. If you were only shown tenderness when you were hurt, you may have learned to appear in distress to receive care.

Cultural, social, and familial taboos dictate our ways of being. Your shadow consists of your disowned shames and distasteful ways. It specializes in preparing itself in the secret lair of your subconscious, waiting for an opportunity to use its awesome skills to keep your young ego alive.

My shadow was formed by being pushed and pulled with conditional love, creating an anxious and insecure parental attachment. When my shadow is in charge, I cycle on a tireless loop between rebelling angrily and aiming to please. I push love away while anxiously wanting to be enfolded and protected. I ignore pain by counting my blessings.

Your shadow may act like an angry beast, sly and tricky, invisible or demanding of attention. It may lash out against too many limits and rules, or it may be flaky. It may use magical thinking to bypass responsibility. It might find you in jail to reinforce the message that you're not safe to be around others. It may want love at any cost to your body. Your shadow can convince you that you will never be enough so it's best not to risk failure, rejection, or making a fool of yourself.

UNRELENTING VOICES

It is perfectly ordinary to hear voices inside our heads. Engaging in self-dialogue does not indicate mental unwellness. Being prompted by your inner thoughts and memories to feel or act is not the same as being given audible directives to harm oneself or others.

The sounds of your shadow will vary. Each aspect—inner critic, judge, taskmaster, dictator, boss, lieutenant, perpetual student, saboteur, victim, rebel—has a favorite voice to use on you. These members of your inner board of trustees are relatively powerless innocents who had little control over their early environments. They found a role inside of your mind to keep you safe.

For fun, think of these inner players like kids in the middle school band. Remember how cacophonous that sounded? They're all vying for your ear while you stand at the front of the stage trying to get them to harmonize.

Your shadow has a lot to say. A large majority of its commentary is negative, because it is full of fear. This is not to get you to exercise positive thinking, but to encourage you to understand what that kid blasting away on the saxophone is going through at home, and generate empathy for that little one with the piccolo, nearly undetectable at the back of the room.

The loudest voices get the most attention, so you must ask yourself what part of your inner child earned a starring role in your personality and what parts of you were better off silent and invisible? What parts of you are you listening to when you feel the lowest? What part of you comes forward when you feel threatened or insecure?

MASKING PAIN

Pain doesn't always present as sadness or victimization. It may present as rage, anger, withdrawal, control, anxiety, depression, illness, dependency, mania, perfectionism, or other afflictions. Your face may scowl or your eyebrows furrow. It may not show itself at all.

To understand what your pain really looks like, begin by observing yourself in stressful or confrontational situations. How do you react in the face of conflict, disappointment, and loss? Do you tend toward resentment? Confusion? Defensiveness? Silence? An open display of sorrow?

Knowing your default settings under stress tells you about the nature of your shadow, which can help you track it. Remember: you were not born with a shadow. It was built by experiencing complex models of interaction that caused you to curb your natural impulses in order to avoid disappointing or displeasing someone close to you. It crystallized in place when it served to protect you with certain behaviors and outward appearances. Shadow works to get your needs met and avoid or control a situation.

Being hurt results in trying to prevent it from happening again, although what often happens is we end up re-enacting the circumstances. Recognizing this pattern means you'll someday want to take off the mask to shift what you're painfully re-living.

In conflict, what does your expression and posture reflect? Where do you hear yourself becoming confused or childlike? Try going to a mirror when you feel triggered to get a sense for what masks you put on without knowing it.

EARS UP FOR SELF-TALK

Develop the skill to hear yourself in a shadow state. In the same way emotions register on your face, your voice will reveal where your shadow is hanging you up.

To tune into what's agitated within you, consider your outward expressions. What do you say out loud, in texts, or in emails when you feel most rattled? Do you write volumes of angry novels or talk in an uninterruptable blue streak? Do you quietly mutter, trying to unravel your inner chaos? Try to discern how you'd like to speak and be heard.

Do you write in all caps? There could be a need to control the conversation. Do you express sorrow with emojis? Maybe your sadness pre-dates being verbal. Do you wait for months or years building courage to tell someone how you feel? Maybe your shadow is showing you that it wasn't safe to speak about feelings when you were young. If you don't get a response, do you drive to the offender's home and bang on the door, possessed by an overwhelming desire for acknowledgment of your suffering? Is it possible you were silenced as a child and rage surfaces when that happens now?

Record yourself when experiencing big emotions. Say what you really want to say in the moment. Listen for clues about how you are asking for permission or aiming to please. Spend time reflecting on your modes of expression to better understand the parts of you that have been activated. Hearing your shadow speak has the power to connect you to your early fears and needs in moments of tension.

NO PLACE LIKE HOME

Your shadow's presence may take you by surprise. A favorite stage for your shadow is in your close, personal relationships—such as you have with partners and family members.

An undetected shadow halts the progress of uncomplicated communication. It creates chaos and confusion by shutting you down or growing you big to prepare to fight. It can cloud the facts of a situation with thoughts of the painful past. Your internal small, scared child can opt to burst out of the closet swinging, or take shelter in it to insulate you from the kind of pain that still lives in your memory. Try to sense whether your bruised soldier within is taking measures to keep you safe at home, where you are supposed to feel the safest.

It can be challenging to communicate in a moment of stressful conflict, but vocalizing what has come to the surface is empowering. This process requires a check-in—a quick inventory of what lives in the body that is informing the reaction. Developing the muscle to check in helps more mature forms of consciousness be the lead voice on the matter.

In the beginning, you can implement your healing plan by stopping the conversation or action with an acknowledgment. You might say, "My shadow's coming up" or "I'm feeling triggered and need space to tend to myself."

When you can identify injury and notice when you're feeling an overwhelming need to prevent additional pain from occurring, you can ask your loved ones for space and understanding. It's important to recognize that restoring your inner health is up to you, especially in the midst of your closest relationships.

CALL IT WHAT IT IS

Everyone has a shadow. It's part of who we complex, thinking mammals are by nature.

What we see of a person is the tiny tip of their very large iceberg. Under the surface is an enormous mountain of experiences—memories and forgotten sufferings held inside the body. Trauma, thought loops, fear, anxiety, guilt, shame, abuse, and confusion are all influencers in your mind's playing field. When possessed by nonconscious influences, it can be very challenging to be realistic. Many memories were stored long before the prefrontal cortex was fully developed, which happens between twenty-five and thirty years of age. The prefrontal cortex has been called "the wise old owl" by educators because it guides and governs your ability to think and react beyond your primal fear reactions of fight, flight, and freeze.

Working with your shadow allows the unspoken, unacknowledged parts of you to become illuminated by your thinking self so you can be clear about what you're made up of. Curiosity for what you're carrying helps you to do something with pain that hasn't gone away: cultivate the skills to override your shadow's influence and move the energy safely.

It doesn't work to hold it hostage or deny it. That's what happened with your original feelings that got you here. Your ability to hide your shadow is what it is counting on, so it can continue working to keep you feeling invulnerable and safe. The cost in adulthood is intimacy, closeness, trust, and security with others. Call your shadow by name when it rises up and take productive and healing action.

DISSOCIATION

If you can imagine that parts of your psyche can become fragmented by traumatic experiences, perhaps you can imagine that it is possible to reintegrate them back into your whole being.

Sometimes trauma happens in one big blow, as in a car accident. Sometimes it slowly wears you down over time, as an emotionally abusive caregiver might. In both cases, trauma can cause the victim to dissociate from the body (and its sensations) to defend against feeling the pain of what is happening. Dissociation is our nonconscious ability to put away our needs, thoughts, and feelings in order to survive. It has been described as a phenomenon of leaving the body. Dissociating causes a disconnect from the body in the present moment and hinders sensations.

This trauma response happens not just early in life, but any time a trauma is unbearable. When someone is rendered powerless, they are resigned to surrender. The young, ill, and elderly may be at higher risks of being put in a position where power is not shared with them.

The human soul is tenacious, able to live through internal and external trauma while continuing to function as expected. If you feel fragmented or as if only part of you is present in your body, seek a healer or therapist who can listen to, and perhaps coax back, the aspects that had to seek refuge out of your body. Healing modalities such as shamanic or somatic therapies, EMDR, and brainspotting can help with identifying lost sensitivities in order to integrate them back into the whole.

GUILT & SHAME

When guilt and shame rise up like steam from emotional swamplands, know that it's all part of creating potential for discharging toxic patterns. You may find that you want to make amends to yourself and others. Your children may benefit from hearing that you're aware of how you've mishandled them as a result of past pain—and your plan to go forward (in age-appropriate terms). You may want to talk with your lover about where your shadow shows up in your relationship.

If it helps, think of guilt as feeling badly about a mistake and wanting to make it right. Take heart in what sex and relationship therapist, Julie Jeske, says: *"Intimacy happens when we make repairs."* Remember that a painful past causes us to make mistakes in relationship. If repairs can be made, there is a reward: growing closer and rebuilding trust by re-bonding after a disruption.

Shame maintains a belief that you are bad and there's nothing that can be done about it. This is untrue and the ultimate show-stopper. The theory that a child can be born a "bad seed" is outdated and toxic, and if you allow it, your shadow will have a field day acting out the pain that exists under this label. Promptly address issues of toxic shame. The work of Brené Brown helps millions of individuals suffering its crippling effects.

It helps to know that everyone has a shadow, that you are not the only one carrying the burden of feeling bad. It's an essential part of all of us. However, it can't diminish the quality of your relationships when you're actively aware of how it's working and determined to take responsibility.

SABOTAGE

The shadow has an objective: you SAFE and SECURE at all costs. That doesn't sound like such a bad thing. However, the nonconscious shadow is like a baby rattlesnake that exhausts all available venom to protect itself rather than reacting with just what is needed to manage a situation. For us, it's stress hormones.

If this is how you wield your shadow, you'll be unable to respond to stressful situations in a manner that fits what is happening. If pressed, it will throw everything under the bus in order to fulfill its purpose and discharge or shove down the energy.

Sometimes a shadow wants to be compensated in other ways: by getting into trouble, getting caught, getting away with something, or being held accountable. Sometimes it seeks to repeat the patterns set up in early childhood. It may look for ways to push other people away to confirm that you are indeed all alone. It may be greedy for fame because being seen as important fulfills a deep and insatiable insecurity, a hunger so profound it will harm others to obtain it.

It is deep work to discover what motivates your shadow and where it comes from. When we are very honest with ourselves, the ashamed, anxious, insecure child inside can come forward and be seen. Shadow can take off its big, scary costume and be vulnerable in your lap for re-parenting the way you needed to be treated originally.

You do not have to throw anyone under the bus or inject them with fatal amounts of venom anymore, yourself included. You do not need to hide in a shell like a snail or turn invisible.

You can cultivate a more mature habit of assessment and response that will suit your adult needs.

FEEL IT TO HEAL IT

Unacknowledged, untended emotions such as frustration, anger, sadness, grief, fear, guilt, and rage circle around inside of us seeking a landing strip to touch down on. I daresay it can feel downright grounding to project big emotions onto our closest people.

It can be jarring to be besieged by unexpected feelings. Whether expressed outwardly (explosive) or turned inward (implosive), the results can be destructive.

If your family model expressed explosive emotions, you might also. If the parent with the most influence over you dissociated or repressed their feelings, you might have imprinted those methods, or their polar opposites, if that's what worked best to neutralize the space. What we know about maturation and development is that continuing to use our nonconscious, reflexive, default settings from childhood is equivalent to driving with a learner's permit well into adulthood. That is to say, we may still be using certain emotional techniques because we haven't developed other age-appropriate options.

It is no longer distasteful or disapproved of to express emotions. Sanctioned emotions, such as anger, are no longer the only choice. There is a wide spectrum of ways to understand our feelings and even more to describe them. People today are open to talking about feelings, which is very different from decades ago. There remains a hardwired idea, among my generation and the one before me, that our more complex or negative feelings are unacceptable. This belief is fading, thankfully. A big part of uncovering the riches of your interior world involves disclosing the truth about what it was like for you, and being responsive to others in the same position.

HOW YOU KNOW

When examining your deep interior spaces, and wondering whether your shadow is at the wheel, you will need to rely on your intuitive best guess. The shadow relies on its ability to fool you. It believes it knows what you need and not your higher consciousness. It is downright wily and will try blame-shifting and gaslighting first you, then others. It may wait for your health and resources to be compromised before it makes a big fuss. As you would with a child who is trying to do anything except what it needs to most, you can promise it that you will stay with it patiently through this process.

Another giveaway that shadow is having its way with you is your use of absolutes: never, always, everyone, nobody—universal terms that reinforce aloneness and dismay, and that are usually unprovable. Shadow complains quite a bit. Often there is a deeper need beneath the superficial need, asking to be noticed.

A clue that your shadow is at work is if your emotions present with childlike features. Recovery programs and Al-Anon™ use acronyms to help them stay conscious. One that works well in my home for both adults and children is HALT: hungry, angry, lonely, and tired. If you are any of these things, and puzzling over whether shadow is afoot, (while it makes a compelling argument about why you should fight, fly, or freeze), remember how children act and sound when they feel this way. If you tend to your basic needs for nourishment, emotional space, breath, the ear of a friend, and rest, the insight will come. When doing depth healing work, we can be more emotionally depleted. For those healing trauma and childhood wounds, it is okay not to know all of the answers and next actions right away, and to meet basic needs before trying to wring out wisdom.

AN EYE FOR TREASURE

Sometimes we think we know ourselves, how we move through the world, what brings us pleasure, anxiety, love, fear, joy. Until we dig into the shadows, we cannot actually see the whole map of our being.

Listening to stories of women throughout my adulthood, I've come to see their strengths in me. Their abilities to overcome adversity present possibility. I've been braver to goldmine my depths for the hidden gems I didn't know were there, particularly interested in how my rejected parts could be assets. It's exciting to return to childhood and adolescence to pick up what I left behind there.

Diving deeply into your healing process is a way to honor what happened that created you as you are today. Traumatic and hurtful events that shaped you recall pain, but they also reclaim wonder. Their teachings make us aware of what we don't need to tolerate, and also what we can build more tolerance for. To see in ourselves what we abhor in others strengthens our ego and our relationships, and sturdies us for life.

While shadow work can feel heavy and high-commitment, it is rewarding work. Deep-dish soul excavation unearths your instincts and revitalizes your intuition, unburies them from the programming heaped on you, and builds resilient confidence. If you interface with something that you don't want to remember about yourself, turn it over and view it upside-down. Get a good look under the hood and see what's helped this engine stay running despite how it's been run down, neglected, inappropriately fueled, and inadequately lubricated.

Perspective broadens the mind and makes room for acceptance.

EXCRUCIATING VULNERABILITY

On a path of healing, you are sure to come into contact with the squeezing feeling of being in a bottleneck. Healing cannot be rushed. It cannot be a productive process without a commitment to feel vulnerable again. Like the transit through the vessels we came through into the light of the world, it is a rite of passage that takes time and sacred tending. Healing is for the hearty.

Interfacing with shadow involves seeing your antagonist in contrast to your protagonist—for me, my obsessive control-monger, Darth Vader, to my do-gooding warrior, Luke Skywalker. The things that you find most distasteful about yourself are occupying the most cells in your inner dungeons. As you look into the recent past, you will see where you have caused wreckage. As you look further back, you will see a child with unmet needs for care, boundaries, limits, structure, freedom, sacredness, vitality, encouragement, access, education, space, celebration, love, shelter, power, spiritual support, nourishment, PROTECTION, and so much more.

It's agonizing to see yourself as an innocent with unfulfilled needs and dreams. No one may know what was the hardest for you to carry. You may not have words for the pain you've felt or the tragedy you've experienced and witnessed. Vulnerability is your constant companion as you face having had to pack away your innocence and armor up to be able to make it in the world.

UNBEARABLE DISCOMFORT

Like excruciating vulnerability, shadow work can bring up discomfort. I believe modern humans have an unusual obsession with comfort. I often hear people say that they are not comfortable with something or someone, indicating that ease is the first priority. I would like to see a shift in language and intention here to be more representative of what is actually going on. Does comfort mean one doesn't wish to be confronted by certain sensations or thoughts? If you find that you're seeking comfort, check in with your ability to have confrontation. Shadow work most certainly asks you to be confrontational with yourself as you examine your habits. Acknowledging discomfort allows you to identify the unsettling matter inside of you that has been stirred.

Anti-racism conversations scare me silly, because engaging in them will likely stir up unbearable guilt or shame about participating in and benefitting from a system that I often feel powerless to change. It takes courage to show up for what matters.

When uncomfortable, ask yourself, "What am I afraid is going to happen?" When I answer this question, I find that I am usually willing to experience the consequences of confrontation, rather than miss an opportunity to grow and learn.

Anything that helps an individual heal, stretch, and grow requires confrontation: updating a previous belief, reworking old patterns that no longer serve, overhauling your spiritual systems, implementing an elimination diet. Comfort is not a companion of change.

Humans are stronger than we give ourselves credit for. Shadow work is tough, but it's not worse than what you've already been through.

FALSE COMFORT

When we feel a deep longing or missing, we will try to fill the gaps with pseudo-comforts and quick-fix pleasures. The treats and thrills that we indulge in while we are in a shadow state allow us to perpetuate the myth that we are taking care of ourselves. The truth is that we are soothing ourselves in ways we learned that provide a brief respite, without addressing the underlying cause of suffering that leads to the need for shadow pleasures. Acting in this way is a cover-up for what we really want more of. Often it is intimacy, closeness, peace, rest, or to be worry-free for just a little while.

Finding ways to medicate or soothe the underlying suffering turns easily to addiction and/or obsession in some people. At that point, we have to find reasons to defend and excuse behaviors that keep us stagnant or dissociated, tolerating abuse and neglect from ourselves and others. Living with an undercurrent of shame becomes normal.

What we feel shame about, we will often try to express in acceptable ways. It shows up as false humility, self-deprecation, or constantly apologizing. An individual with bulimia will hide binges. An alcoholic will find a way to function and appear as an upstanding citizen. A sex addict will spend more time in fantasy than reality.

Self-soothing is normalized to the point of daily habituations: coffee before work, drinks after work, checking out on the weekends. Our needs become more difficult to accommodate as we reach outside for more ways to comfort the persistent sense of dissatisfaction.

SELF-LOATHING

Coming to terms with your shadow's effects on others can make you ashamed enough to want to get it off of you in a hurry. Shame is heavy and low-vibration. It is the iron boot on the throat of the human condition. Finding yourself unable to deny your part in someone else's pain or the state of your life can tempt you to stop this process altogether. You cannot unknow what you're responsible for once you have pinned down what the issue is. It will not get back in the trunk. So how do you live with the deplorable consequences of your actions? I can report that blaming others will get you nowhere—I've tried it, with short-term results, at best.

Here's the thing. The shadow cannot be pruned off like a dead tree limb. It cannot be amputated. To want it gone is dangerous to the soul. I cringe to hear people claim they intend to kill their egos: they have confused the function of the ego with egocentrism. These are critical parts of the psyche that simply haven't matured yet. Your psyche worked very hard from a young age to create its expert survival mechanisms. It is not the fault of your shadow that your life or relationships are in a shamble. It is part of fully developing.

It can feel defeating to discover that you are the one responsible for your suffering. To self-punish is to allow the shadow to again misdirect your mission. You do not need more ways to suffer just as you're trying to find relief and create accountability.

When you realize you've had a part in hurting someone, you have the power (responsibility) to make amends. When you realize you've been hurting yourself, you can track the pattern and offer compassion. No amount of punishing yourself will ever result in peace.

A WILDERNESS OF THREATS

Shadow work is mostly a solo enterprise. Processing emotions with a therapist helps immensely, but you will be the one to put yourself to bed at night with your thoughts.

When exploring the deeper aspects of how your past informs your present, you may have thoughts about yourself that are frightening. It may seem appealing to numb out or distract yourself in order to cope with what you're being shown. It may be tempting to let your shadow fully take the reins and take you on a long, depressing ride downhill. Note where you are choosing to become mired in the pain and where you are able to see it objectively, as a loving parent would observe a child. Take frequent breaks and go slowly.

Remember that thoughts are not always reality, but they do generate feelings. The thoughts you have may or may not determine how you feel about yourself, but they do not always determine the truth about how you will proceed. To move forward with strength, talk to yourself encouragingly with the love of an adult who is seeking to understand their child. Do not repeat the heavy-handedness, abandonment, entitlement, or neglect that you were raised with. Do it differently.

If shadow work triggers symptoms that require attention, check in with your coping skills before you continue on. Have a trusted close friend, elder, or family member nearby for support as you sift through your history and try to see the forest as more than a cluster of scary trees.

THE RAGE OF SELF-BETRAYAL

When you project your anger out onto another person, there is one part that's angry about being a victim of unfair circumstances, and another part that's angry because you're in the situation to begin with.

Betrayal of innocence and personal violations leave a victim feeling exploited, unprotected, and vulnerable. Anger is a fitting suit of armor for violations. It is justified rage. It can heal when there's action behind it. A boundary that says, "ENOUGH," that is energized by follow-through usually does the trick.

Sustained, unprocessed anger stresses your body's systems. Emotions are cleansing when they move through the tissue and voice. Anger can be a powerful motivator for change, yet it's also the fire that burns us out, inflames our bodies, and eventually causes serious medical conditions. Anger cannot help if it's trapped internally or exists in a pattern of explosion/retreat.

You might find it helpful to take fifty-one percent responsibility for your part, (enough to do something about it), and honor that forty-nine percent of it had nothing to do with you. Your accountability must be higher, or you're left powerless to change.

Healing happens *with* accountability. As adults with traumatic pasts, we cannot get above our own shadows and begin living on our terms while we deny how we are self-betraying in this moment. We will blame, shame, and make others responsible as we toil in the poison of stagnant anger.

BEG, BORROW & STEAL

We only need to steal when we think we can't get what we truly need any other way. Stealing, sneaking, and manipulating are tricks that come from not taking the time to assess what the need really is. I still catch myself "borrowing time" or "sneaking in pleasure" because I still carry an archaic, lingering guilt about meeting my own needs. There are children to consider, for heaven's sakes, and hard work is what pays the bills.

When I was a teenager, my girlfriend and I pocketed lipsticks from the local drugstore. The risk seemed worth it. Our parents assumed that our motivations were to see what we could get away with, which may have been partly true. Ripe to explore, however, is what it was like to have self-absorbed mothers practicing addiction who resented and feared our development. Neither was present to our budding femininity or our craving for their upliftment. Did we resort to stealing our beauty to assert it?

Teenagers don't always know how to name what they need. It may not be safe to confide in a family member who is unlikely to respond with care.

As I sifted through these memories looking for what motivated my behavior, I saw that my mother's needs as a teen had been less met than mine. Her inability to greet my puberty stage with care was understandable given her unhealed trauma and neglect. A parent's damage is easily passed down through generations and may change form. It's as if it must mutate a bit to remain less detectable.

As adults, we can refuse to beg, borrow, sneak, steal, or otherwise contort to get our needs met. It's simpler to learn what you need and provide it.

OBJECTIFICATION

Do you notice where you treat people like objects, game-pieces, trophies, dolls, baby makers, pleasure machines, rescuers, soldiers, banks, heroes, servants, grunts? Fetishizing others is part of the culture we live in, and we all participate in it.

Children are not here to make us look good or feel proud. They are not cute little mini versions of us. They're here to learn how to be decent people, by our example. Women do not exist to be arm candy or to serve their mates sexually or at the expense of their dignity. Men are not for riding up on white horses to save damsels or to provide household handiness. Black and brown people are not here to sweep up after us while we do needlepoint on fainting couches.

Hubris and projections have created a very poor quality of life for the objectified. When we believe others and the earth to be inferior, here solely for making our lives easy, comfortable, and convenient, we perpetuate a generational cycle of objectification.

We who live in colonized nations built on genocide and slavery practice this deeply ingrained habit daily. Profiting from the oppression of others does not lend to liberty. It has become a nonconscious reflex to expect benefits without sharing labor.

When we objectify a person, race, or gender, we ignore their humanity, snatch away their human rights, and file them beneath us. Subjugating another for what they do for us is self-serving and self-destructive. It erodes the dignity of fellow humans while diminishing our integrity.

To fully engage in inner work with your shadow, prepare to help repair the culture by enlisting in the service and liberation from the harmful impact of objectification.

WHAT THE SHADOW IS HUNGRY FOR

Your shadow is hungry for power in the form of control. It doesn't know how to be responsible with the power it wields over your adult life. It is young and immature, and it represents the underdeveloped part of you that runs on an undercurrent of subtle angst—waiting for the next shoe to drop. It is hungry for the opportunity to jump in and protect you.

It is nourished by whatever will perpetuate the cycle it was formed in. It sounds rather parasitical, but it's actually the neglected child inside each of us, acting out its big, anxious feelings in the only way it knows how. When you view your shadow as your child, the adult you are now can comfort and protect it from making irreversible choices.

If you take your shadow out for ice cream, it doesn't need to be twelve scoops on a chocolate-dipped waffle cone with caramel sauce and a cherry. The adult in you must be in charge. You are the one with the wisdom of experience and access to common sense.

Shadow has a valuable voice and an impeccable memory for details. It serves you so that you will never be hurt again. Shadow doesn't realize you're an adult now, and that you're using advanced technology from developed places in the brain that didn't exist when it was adapting to circumstances beyond your control.

Feed your shadow your most precious time and awareness. Feed it compassion and understanding. Feed it sanctuary in community, and also solitude it can rest in. Feed it dialogue unclouded by fears and overprotection. Feed it your wholeness and your richness of perspective and healing introspection. Take it to an all-you-can-eat buffet of creative options.

INJURED PRIDE

The companion to this book, *Boundaries & Protection: Honoring Self, Honoring Others*, discusses the importance of ego strength and how to develop it.

In the beginning of any process intended for housekeeping of the soul, fragile egos will be challenged. The reason we have wobbly egos is because we nonconsciously overprotect ourselves from the truth and cannot withstand hearing feedback about our behavior. This can be remedied—*with consistent practice at responding to feedback with maturity*. Fragile egos can only persist when we allow our unhealed wounds to respond defensively to criticism.

We seem to be having a social epidemic of fragility. Most people do not want to hear opinions about how they're showing up in the world or how their commentary is biased. That would mean we're not perfect, right? Aiming for perfection is a dangerous game that makes hearing feedback impossible.

Ego strength is not armor made of pain or a graceful mask for insecurities and fear. It isn't pompous or uptight. A person with ego strength is a gem—humble and willing to listen, take in feedback, think on it, and get back to you. They do not crumple into a heap, hide, or cancel you. They make efforts to come to resolution.

Critique is worthwhile and helps us grow. It is valuable even when it stings. There is often a grain of truth in what comes at us, and at the very least we'll know where our vulnerabilities are. It's a fine exercise in listening for your shadow.

Some feedback is not feedback, but assaulting, abusive, and harmful trash-talk, and does not need to be a part of your life. It is not our duty to negotiate with another's shadow.

RELEASING TOXICITY

Having zero tolerance for another's pain doesn't build strong relations. What helps is setting limits on how you interact with their shadow. You can create terms and conditions that generate productive conversations.

There are toxic ways to express our pain: overreacting, explosive or implosive behaviors, addictions, obsessions, cravings, self-betrayal, doing harm, overworking, distraction, self-medicating, numbing out, recoiling, isolating, neglecting, blaming, power-tripping, inability to take responsibility or apologize, keeping secrets, coercion, collusion, manipulation, and more.

There are as many ways to share personal pain consciously: with transparency, vulnerability, accountability, humility, with a counselor and friends, by grieving your losses. Taking responsibility for how your suffering is expressed to others takes practice. It makes a world of difference to have a patient person in your life when you're learning to be more conscious in relationship. Breaking patterns and adulting is necessary, but it can feel exhausting at times.

In relationships, you can dismiss someone from your life because you don't like how they express their shadow, but check in with your tolerance level first. Doing your own shadow work helps you to be stronger to witness those in earlier stages. Is the person in question on a path of inner wellness? Cultivate an open dialogue with loved ones by normalizing terms like shadow, trigger and inner child. Create an atmosphere for richer processing and healing.

There is connection to be had by showing you care about what it's like for others. Some people in your life will not want, or be able to grow beyond toxic shadow expressions. You decide when toxic behavior must be addressed, and if necessary, released.

YES TO THIS HARD JOURNEY

When I began my journey with my shadow, I felt like a deer in the headlights. There was no turning back, and few were there to hold my hand. The events occurring in my life at that time were preparing me for heartiness, though heck if I knew what it would all lead to. I'd become successful at avoiding the backstory of my life, which was bubbling up with a frothy stench.

You may think that you don't have the stomach for facing haunting past hurts. If you're new to healing yourself and feel weary, it's okay to press pause. The shadow is a master at hiding. What it is concealing are your real needs, and it can be challenging to know what to do when you allow them to surface. You get to be the manager of how the process goes. Pace yourself.

Panther sits on the cover of this book to remind you to hunt by night, tending your interior world with care for what deeply nourishes and truly heals you. Healing relies on awareness. Knowing why and how you struggle is half the battle. Communicating truth is one part; making different choices and being brave to see how they work out is another.

You have your lifetime to consider how rich a human life can be on the inside. You are discovering your ability to cope and respond in a way that helps you sparkle with vitality. You are stretching to be able to hold more, help more, and offer understanding to yourself and those around you. You are showing willingness to be whole, seeking peace to replace the undercurrent of subtle anxiety. Stay with it.

ASSIMILATING THE EGO

Your soul is existing and surviving under extreme external pressure to fulfill demands determined by the world around you. It is supported by the landscape within you. A fragile inner landscape doesn't serve your soul or the connection and belonging it yearns for. The knowledge that your darkness and lightness are mutually beneficial enriches the soil in which your soul grows. A cultivated, sturdy inner terrain is regulated by the question of what is beneficial for the overall growth and development of individual and collective consciousness.

Humans have been mediating the space between the heavens and the earth for tens of thousands of years. This process became amplified when early curiosity evolved into science as we know it today. In order to harmoniously mediate the space between your private inner world and the front you present, you must contend with your ego. What do you want and why do you want it?

A recently individuated person—one who is claiming responsibility for how their inner life functions—will need to resolve issues of motive and reward. Look clearly at the consequences of what occurred early in life that is influencing how you move through the world. When your ego's desires go unquestioned, only a small portion of your potential is being expressed.

As the maturation process evolves, events occur that provide opportunities for introspection and building new roads to wellness. The desire to illuminate the lessons of pain is evidence of willingness to sacrifice ego-fulfilling responses in favor of what can serve the greater journey.

BIAS

Bias is a term used to describe our tendency to be for or against something based on nonconscious conditioning. It forms the foundations of stereotypes, racism, sexism, classism, genderism—all the -isms that create disharmony and imbalance in ourselves and in our world. We all suffer from the effects of our own nonconscious biases, and we all cause suffering because of them. Humans have a strong drive to look for patterns. We have a strong impulse to sort, categorize, and classify.

We are raised and cultured to create false fronts. We are encouraged, even by well-meaning caregivers, to honor family values or the needs of the whole before our own—in other words: to represent. We are rewarded for things that betray our needs, and learn to behave in ways that narrow how we perceive others and the world we live in. We can make repairs to broken ways of thinking and invite in more of what we want: fairness, closeness, bonding, connection, and belonging. Backtrack through the adaptations you made along your life path to see how you made sacrifices to please (or avoid displeasing) the people you relied upon for love, approval, and a sense of belonging. What did you have to do or believe in order to be accepted?

We are also a culture that values specialization—concrete identifications we can be "known for." The aspects of us that are fluid and ambiguous are less valuable in this system. Many see the flaw in this way of thinking, an example is found in movements led by LGBTQIA communities to transcend the gender binary. Leaving rigid internalized concepts behind eliminates nonconscious judgment and generates empathy and tolerance.

WADING THROUGH SWAMPS

Must I dig up the painful past in order to heal? Who will I be when I confront past hurts? Which of my relationships will be affected and how? Will working to heal myself be like poking a hornet's nest?

It's okay to move your focus away from micro-analyzing your childhood and onto identifying what you want to replace triggered or uncompassionate responses to life's curve balls. When you begin to see how your shadow has impacted you, tension and shame can subside as prevailing forces in your life. Despite the mistakes made during my childhood, it has helped immeasurably to realize that what I really want is relationships I can count on. To start, I need a few good laps to lay my head in now and then. I also want to be a safe lap for those I'm close with. One major task can be to discover what makes you safe for others to confide in and want to bond with, and what helps you want to bond with others.

When in a healing process, it is imperative to let loved ones in on the news. Tell them you are healing something old that is impacting you in ways you want to change. Tell them your emotions may be closer to the surface and that it's sometimes like being up to your neck in quicksand. Tell them you may not be very available as you identify what's been draining you in order to turn it into vital energy. Let your people know that you're down in the muck finding out what isn't working for you anymore and that you'll be sure to report back soon.

EXISTENCE INSECURITY

Soul work is made even more challenging by the plagues of modern existence. These are most certainly The Insecure Times. Perhaps they are no more so than any other period, but I do believe we're airing our insecurities in a public way more than ever. Perfectionism, rejection, sadness about the past, and anxiety about the future are claiming space and causing us to seek false forms of confidence.

All who pioneered modern existential thought were fore-fathers, that is, white-haired, white men—not unlike those in power today. The predominant misogyny of their writings and teachings still informs our governments and educational institutions. The world we live in is forcefully influenced by the thoughts and ideas of the long-dead European males that brought us nihilism and manifest destiny. These overculture shadows leave little room for spiritual matters such as seeking out a subtle current of peace to balance the chaos of our ever-evolving minds and technologies. We're far too busy dreading, fearing, and trying to make sure we have life insurance and a retirement plan for uncertain times ahead to cultivate new and equitable philosophies to live by.

What brings you security? Name three anchoring thoughts or ideas of your very own about your life and death that bring you a sense of peace and freedom of spirit.

BEAUTIFUL MESS

For each influence of shadow within you there is an illuminated counterpart. Each benefit from expressing our shadows nonconsciously has a cost. Each unearned privilege has an unpaid debt. Each major decision has a devil's advocate. Sounds like a lot to keep track of.

Reaction, in Newtonian physics, is the precisely equal force that opposes any action. The stronger we love, the more we fear losing it. The more light that shines on an object, the darker the shadows that will be cast behind it. The depth of night isn't in conflict with the brightness of day but made more beautiful by the contrast we experience. We perceive the world around us through contrast, but often fail to honor the aspects we find most challenging about it.

What do you have to work with? A major trauma with a timestamp? An unyielding weight that wore you down over time and hunched your shoulders forward? A case of being at the wrong place at the wrong time? An unbearable shame about what you weren't able to do right? An undercurrent of never-enoughness? No roadmap from those who were supposed to guide and set you up for success?

Whatever the sack on your back contains, there is a remedy. When right medicine is applied, it is a salve that regenerates your cells and breathes new life into you. The depth of your pain is equal to your potential for brightness. Self-healing exposes the tragedy of your pain, and boundless beauty is revealed in the process.

JINNI IN A BOTTLE

There is a very old story from the Arabian Nights about a fisherman who catches a jinni (or "genie") in his fishing net early one morning. The jinni has been captive inside a copper bottle sealed with lead for many centuries by a king who betrayed him. While inside for the first hundred years, he vowed to shower the one who releases him with eternal riches. The second, with immeasurable wealth. The third century, he vowed to grant three wishes to the person who freed him. By the fourth, his rage at being imprisoned had grown so intense, he would only allow the person who uncorked his bottle a choice of how to die.

Our shadows aren't demons, but they can be held for a very long time. Meanwhile, we quietly make strategic vows to get even. We prepare to weaponize our pain without realizing that's what we're doing. It may not show as wrath like jinni's, it could be withdrawal from love, abandonment, a drunken bender, anger toward a specific group, or self-harming behaviors. What we really want is to have our whole story understood and to be accepted anyway.

When the smoke of past suffering rises up, it can be appealing to make someone pay. The built-up energy seeks to be discharged. This is understandable and also a directive from your injured shadow child. We need to be more creative at releasing old energy than channeling misdirected revenge. Vindictive behavior comes from shadow hurts. Personal power comes from recognizing this connection and choosing a response that serves the mature version of you.

TRAUMA BONDING

Dancing with the shadows of our loved ones is ill-advised. This is where our relationships act out shadows on the familial stage. We humans have a way of falling in love with each other's wounds—for better and for worse. Listen to the story of someone newly smitten and there will often be sparks of how the other is seen as the one who will complete them or is a perfect fit.

Trauma bonding is a phrase that describes the chemistry and magnetism our shadows experience together. It is the powerful reason behind loitering in toxic, abusive relationships. There may be short periods of peace or euphoria, but dramatic emotional swings are the hallmark.

The shadow is starving for its unmet needs for connection and belonging to be fulfilled, and we will make many compromises to satisfy it. We will sacrifice our safety, sanity, health, and peace to try to make a relationship work. When a foundation is built on agony and the unhealed aspects of childhood, it will eventually begin to crumble when connection and belonging are perceived as lost. A relationship cannot sustain itself on wounds that appear during conflict and ordeals.

Our personal work as individuals determines what kind of foundation we can build our relationships on. It is painful to leave a toxic relationship. Blaming the other person for unsavory surface behaviors shortchanges the wisdom and healing that can result from the experience. Examine the wounded part in them that spoke so powerfully to the wounded part in you and accept your role. Soften the edges of your shadow when it seeks to punish them for not delivering on promises. Release fantasies that others can heal what must be mended by you.

GRIEVING HEALS THE SHADOW

Grief is greatly under-revered. Paid leave isn't offered to emotionally process the loss of a loved one. It's most certainly not provided for healing the fractures of early development. It nearly requires a mental breakdown for us to claim the time we need to transform pain into acceptance. Can you recall an event in your life when you would have benefitted from time, money, and/or energy to honor your suffering? This is unavailable to most. Our society might break down entirely if we all pause to grieve. We must find ways to do it anyway.

Grief's role in your healing process is to allow hurt, disappointment, rage, disbelief, and sorrow to move through your body. Trapped emotions create disharmony. They are firmly lodged and sticky. Examine your heartbreaks, the canyons left by emotions that carved you like the Rio Grande. What stories are held in the caverns? What floods have you never allowed to come, for fear they wouldn't stop?

By any means necessary, we must take ownership of what we carry. The ghosts of ungrieved pain haunt our inner halls, project onto our loved ones, clog our heart valves, and suck lubrication right out of our joints. Untended, their pressing messages and desperate pleas for flow slow forward movement.

I set aside time in the slower, darker seasons of autumn and winter to inventory the sufferings I cannot process in real-time. Consider writing in your journal, building an altar, or making a card to honor the medicine of each of your pains.

SLOWLY SIFTING GEMS

Answers and wisdom will not come flowing in at once like a waterfall on your thirsty willingness to heal. Healing multiple wounds and influences requires that you admit yourself into a rehabilitation period while life continues to make demands. Delving into shadows raises enthusiasm for the work to get done, so you can move on with life in a better way. After decades of sifting and sorting, shadows still come up every day for me. This is not a process that becomes perfect or complete. There can be no obsessing and needing to have answers—the shadow retreats when pressed, or it finds new ways to be tricky.

When I was a child, I loved playing in the dirt. I could sit for hours in the soft alkaline powder of the San Joaquin Valley. I could draw and write in it, mound it up, pat it down with my small brown hands, and lose myself in its mystery. Healing deep cuts in my family line feels like this. I am a student of my inner world's complexity. In fact, soil is a metaphor for the soul for me. You see, not much would grow in that alkaline desert I played in—not without lots of fertilizer and commercial water. As an adult, I love learning about permaculture: the art of using dying organic matter to transform infertile soil.

This is the point where I remind you to stay the course. Let the arc of time help you get through your reflection and grieving process. Don't rush to turn it all around.

What you're shedding is compost for what you're growing.

MORE PRECIOUS

The medicine of wounds is a journey in which the map is revealed as you go along. Patiently acknowledge your earlier sufferings that have stagnated from denial. It takes time and emotional bandwidth to become aware of, and appreciate, what you didn't know about. Think of it like a conversation with someone you admire who just dug deep and dazzled you with their honesty and vulnerability. You are cultivating a rich inner life by understanding how you came to be and how you are overcoming.

When you encounter a vein of gold hidden in the composite rock of Self, you don't have to do anything with it. You don't need to extract it, exploit it, profit from it, or medicate it. You don't need to show it to others if you don't want to. Your knowing belongs exclusively to you, and you will know how and when to present it to others, if that is what's needed.

What gold are you seeking by examining your shadow? How can you shift your thoughts from external gain to internal richness? What do you wish to hold privately or keep sacred? In becoming intimate with your injuries, you are befriending your innermost self. You will be able to trust yourself to have a safe interior dialogue until you become more ready to share with others.

REPARENTING THE NEGLECTED CHILD

Working with your shadow stirs up unhealed wounds from childhood and often triggers overreactions. Something tenacious at the root wants to be in charge: to protect, to preserve, to shelter us from potential disturbance.

It is a jackpot of a discovery when we can identify the moments in childhood that made a significant impact on our operational systems. It may not seem logical to celebrate the painful traumas of our early years as a treasure chest of information until we integrate the love we have for our innocence back into the whole self. Disruptions to our innocence cannot be allowed to be in charge of our adult lives.

We hear the term "inner child" tossed around—perhaps so much so that it has lost its warmth and appeal. We hear people talking about their inner child in the third person: "My little girl gets scared and goes into hiding when you yell." This is a disownment of what ultimately empowers us. I prefer how a therapist friend phrased it: "Part of me wants to run away and another part of me wants to stay and stand up for myself."

Which "part" is the child and which "part" is the adult? We are the construction of all of the things that have happened to us, including becoming an adult who can recognize when a "part" of us is showing up as a frightened inner child. Power and responsibility grow when this muscle gets stronger.

When we care about all of our parts, we can willingly re-nurture the inner child. We can pause conflict, internal or external, in order to dialogue with the various injured parts of ourselves. We can make choices based in adultness while honoring the aspects that respond reflexively with fight, flight, or freeze.

CAULDRON OF EMOTIONS

Shadow work brings up the feelings. It stirs up the pot that has been settled and finely separated for a long time. There is a beauty in this messy business because it commands valuable time and attention away from your previous programming. If what comes up feels destabilizing, attend steady appointments with a therapist, healer, or caregiver or check in with a neutral friend until you feel grounded again.

In our home, when an adult's shadow rises and threatens to take over, we go into Aggressive Treatment mode. That means every relational expectation is halted and healing becomes the priority. No one pressures the other into performative action while in the healing process. If you read my previous book on boundaries, you will recall that I suggest wearing a t-shirt emblazoned with I AM IN MY HEALING PROCESS as a reminder. These words are lifesavers because they are a flag to those who love us that we are in it right now and are likely to be unavailable due to the amount of emotional stress and stamina needed, outside of the rigors of daily living, in order to get through.

The heartening news is that we do get through. Committing to your healing is a gift you give yourself and everyone around you. Yes, there will be emotions; some so old you have to laboriously shovel the dust off of them just to see what they are.

Keep stirring. Your vital life depends on it.

EMOTIONAL CONTRACTION

Freedom to move is as important in our mental and emotional processes as it is in our physical ones. In movement practices, open kinetic chain exercises allow your foot or hand to be free to move around. Closed-chain exercises create more security, like an anchor. In yoga, cat-cow is a closed-chain asana (posture) where all limbs are grounded on the mat. Tree pose is open-chain, because only one foot is on the ground while your arms gesture toward the sky and the other foot rests on your leg. Open-chain movement requires balance, confidence, and stability in your core. Closed-chain movement helps when you need to stabilize and secure your form.

Borrowing this concept from movement theory helps to understand what happens with emotions when shadow is activated. In an emotional/mental context, contracting protectively shuts you down and prevents open listening and participation. The emotional body is experiencing a need to "close the chain" and focus on security. You can physically sense the withdrawal of energy due to feeling unsafe. Your body language may give clues about what is arising for you. Withdrawal makes perfect sense when you're in a position of being violated, but it is unnecessary when out of danger. Emotions direct actions. You can be sure that your shadow is trying to protect you if you feel triggered into a corner and unable to respond.

Emotional contraction requires inquiry. A helpful response to an emotional contraction is to identify what's at work when reacting, and name it out loud. Own your part, if any. Know what will help you recover your safety and experiment with "opening your chain" again.

ANCESTRAL WOUNDS

Ancestral wounds are those that have perpetuated through your family lineage and indirectly impacted your development. They are the things we know about our people's sufferings that we did not suffer firsthand. These unsolicited hand-me-downs influence our attitudes, customs, parenting, partnering, and overall vitality and zest for life.

It's been said that the most sensitive person in the family will be able to detect the ancestral wounds in the lineage and have the opportunity to heal them. Many clients I've worked with come to me knowing that they are the ones who will be able to transform the patterns that no longer serve. We can effectively make a healing balm for the broken hearts in our families with our awareness and compassion.

Descendants can feel displacement from the homelands as a subtle sense of being lost, unsafe, or ungrounded. Soil from your people's homelands and meditation on your ancestral lands may help you reconnect and embody your existence.

Ancestral wounds are repetitive-use injuries of our familial psyches. Habitual beliefs and attitudes come sliding through time almost effortlessly. What are some of your family sayings? Who did your family distrust? What are the hard lessons your parents made sure to pass down to you in the name of values?

There are many resources for doing deep healing with your forebears. Try to find a limiting belief in you that is also present for a parent and grandparent. If it's getting in the way of your wellness, imagine yourself breaking through restrictive frameworks with the blessing of your ancestors from beyond. You can reclaim what they had to give up.

SELF-REGULATION

During your healing process, you spend energy taking inventory. Emotions surface that have been buried a long time. Soul work is work. All of the fragments of your original personality that went underground for safety require strength and emotional reserves to integrate.

Prompt yourself to breathe slowly through your nose, taking care not to over-oxygenate as you do when stressed. Rapid breathing increases your heart rate, which causes your body to fight to metabolize the excess oxygen, and that causes anxiety and hyperventilation. By instead creating a restful state, what clinical therapists call "rest and digest," your body and brain will know it's safe to divert energy into the rebuilding of neural pathways and cells. This is especially important for those with PTSD. You can create a space within yourself and your environment where stress is decreased and expectations are low.

Self-regulating is how we calm the amygdala, the part of the brain that hyper-responds to stimulus. A habit of unloading stress in unhealthy ways to displace discomfort is not sustainable.

Consider channeling intense emotions by chopping wood, punching pillows, or doing load-bearing exercises such as lifting weights or moving furniture. Resistance against your joints releases chemicals that send signals to your brain that your organs and hormones need a break and energy will be funneled in a different way. A mantra of "Peace. Be still," or "This too shall pass" is helpful for many.

BELONGING & CONNECTION

I've frequently surveyed people on social media about what they want most, beyond the basic needs of shelter and nourishment. The answers seldom vary. Everyone wants to belong and feel connected. Holding our fullness in reserve keeps us safe in some ways and disconnected in others. Why do you think we suffer from such a phenomenon of isolation and division? Why are studies showing that chronic loneliness is rapidly rising?

One reason is that we don't live with our families anymore. Our households are made up of one or two generations. We have developed a distaste for our parents—their outdated values, judgments, and commentary on our lives. We prefer individualism. This way of being has a shadow, too. Our intolerance of, and inability to co-create a life with, our parents and grandparents are showing us some critical information about our ability to establish agreements. We want freedom, and there's nothing inherently wrong with that. The disadvantage is that we don't have family around for the support, wisdom, and ease they do have to offer.

Among our chosen families of friends and like-minds, there is an element of hesitancy to connect. We're in an evolutionary process of re-learning how to have healthy in-person relationships. What most folks want is to feel safe and secure, to trust, and be held when they feel low. We should not think of ourselves as a burden when going through an ordeal, but that is what we have been conditioned to believe. Be a refuge when you can and ask for a lap to lay your head in when you need it.

THE COLLECTIVE SHADOW

The collective shadow is the one that influences everyone in a society. It exists when accepted beliefs are mistaken for truths. It comes from historical, ecological, political, and economic discord and imbalance.

When reigning political systems, religions, or cultures devalue particular identities, conditions, behaviors, or lifestyle choices they make policies that reject and disown those qualities. An example of a collective shadow is the presence of religious attitudes that condemn differences in class, race, gender, and sexuality beyond their measure of acceptability. Remember that stereotyping, finger-pointing, and stigmas come from fear. They are shadow projections used by those alleging superiority and moral righteousness in order to control.

The insecurity born of the influence of the collective shadow is felt as shame and unworthiness, both in individuals and in groups. It is impossible to feel valuable when ingrained standards require toxic choices to measure up. We see this with fat-shaming by the medical field toward people who do not meet the ideal criteria for size and slut-shaming toward women who are open about their sexuality.

Who sets these standards, and why are they so important to reinforce? Not only should we be questioning where these doctrines came from, but who they serve. Religious establishments and governments may set expectations for their congregations and citizenry, but they must always be appealed and updated as needed.

Let us always question traditions and systems that harm others and hold them accountable to what Carl Jung referred to as "psychic epidemics."

FEAR OF DEATH

Death is perceived as a threat in modern culture rather than a rite of passage. This is problematic. Fears about death can result from a lack of faith about the existence of an afterlife, or a need for assurance about what that will be like if it does exist. It can also stem from fear of physical and emotional pain, and anxiety about having our affairs in order. Regrets and unreconciled relationship issues add to the dilemma, as well as fantasies about longevity.

There's a fine line between fighting for our lives and letting go of what we cannot control. I have not mastered letting go, but I ponder when it's appropriate to resist impending death and when it's right timing to practice acceptance and allow it to unfold. Our relationship to death needs some work.

The fact is that we're all walking toward death from the moment we're born. New life is celebrated. Old life is, at best, made comfortable in hospitals and with pharmaceuticals. Understandably, we do not want to witness or think of loved ones suffering on their way to the other side. But there is something puzzling about palliative care and our desire to prolong the lives of the dying, particularly for the very elderly. When is intervention the best option? Consider that the uninsured and underserved have fewer alternatives.

The business of death is another collective shadow that preys upon the fears of a people obsessed with anti-aging, comfort, and convenience over the very natural process of life's completion. Take the time to imagine your death and tell your loved ones what you'd like, who you'd like to handle your body, and how. Prepare in a way that will give you peace today.

DIVERSIFY

When we move through our lives in well-worn patterns, we have limited perspectives. This is a linear way to approach our lives that results in lifestyle repetitive-use injuries.

It's been my experience that my body expects me to move in a certain way. Squatting down to get the olive oil from the bottom cabinet shows me that my form is unpracticed. My knees crackle in confirmation while my hip sticks in the socket. My range of motion is restricted. My body yearns to move the way I did forty years ago.

We can learn by listening to our bodies and exploring our expectations of them. We want them to continue being open and flexible into mid-life, but if we do not move them outside of their habitual and frontally-adapted gestures, our soft tissues and joints become rigid and immobilized.

Such is life. In a healing process, we expand by asking our emotions and thoughts to move outside their usual range. In our social lives, we can ask ourselves to make different kinds of friends and engage other perspectives, to educate ourselves in the customs of others.

Diversification has never been more possible or more important. Single-purpose ways of being are too restrictive. On some level, the soul knows this. Life becomes lackluster when not inspired to challenge the status quo.

When working with the shadow, skills such as communication and critical thinking are activated. Critical feeling is a term I would like to see adopted into our language as we stretch and move to meet the times. A little ecstatic dance now and again can get things moving in the right direction.

SECURE YOUR BASE

With both feet on the ground, you can root your inner work into the earth beneath you as a practice. I have found no single ritual that has delivered me from my shadow more effectively than staying in my body while confronting it.

Tune into your body. It is your first responder, sending you physical and emotional signals about whether to find the old familiar groove, or engage a state of trusting. There is a slender window of opportunity there to join adult you with your inner child to decide how to respond. Imagine that when the nonconscious shadow is trying to take over, you reach for a mask, a sword, a blanket to cover up with—your suit of armor. Your vulnerability is afraid to be wounded and you have the option to shut down, fight back, run away, control, or dominate so you won't have to feel the pain again. Ramping up to brace for pain is the shadow's way of grabbing the wheel to make sure you don't die. You might ask, "Am I in true danger here?" Compassionately intervening will help you negotiate with the powerful force that is trying so hard to protect you.

You can secure the human form you embody by speaking what's happening out loud to yourself. When engaging in intentional, compassionate self-dialogue, you can allow your higher consciousness to coach you along through a difficulty. "My heart rate is speeding up and I'm not sure why... Is there a reason I feel like I'm in fight, flight, or freeze? What is my nervous system doing? How can I down-regulate before making my next move?"

SPIRITUAL BATTLES

You might think of your internal dilemmas as spiritual battles you are privately fighting inside of yourself. It is a battle with something you've identified that you'd like to change and yet feel powerless to. Internal battles cause internal stress and quarrelsome dialogues. I have a friend who says his wounds are so powerful that each day he has to make a choice first thing in the morning about which side he's going to be on. He is speaking about whether he will be loyal to his distorted beliefs about himself or if he will be a decent human being that moves with care for himself and others. Just sharing this with me relieves the secret pressure he faces.

In relationship, it may feel like a battle to honor agreements, offer transparency, share responsibility, and be there for your loved ones in the ways your conscious self wants you to be. The battle intensifies when a part of you wants one thing and your powerful shadow wants another.

The remedy is to begin with you. What decisions do you have to make to be a decent human being? Must you override a powerful prompt from your injuries to make that choice? Are you denying a need that you can't express because it might be rejected or ridiculed?

People privately believe very corrosive things about themselves. This is shadow taking up a lot of real estate in the mind with a very convincing argument that loyalty to it will keep you safe. Self-destructing and harming others out of loyalty to wounds and wounders is poison.

INTEGRATION

Let's try a less dualistic approach than looking at our shadows as the dark and scary unknown and light as our illuminated consciousness. Darkness is scary. Children are naturally afraid when the lights go down. We are told through folklore and caregivers that darkness is something to be wary of. We are nonconsciously biased against dark things and dark people. This has been catastrophic for over 500 years in North America. In the Americas, "darkness" was represented by the "Merciless Savage Indians," who needed to be subverted or exterminated. During and after that genocide, much of the wealth of the nation was built by the exploitation of black African slaves. Colonized countries are holocaust nations, and it is time to bring that national shadow up for review.

Today we are deeply, unknowingly motivated to fear dark skin and oppress those who have it. The cat's out of the bag about how prevalent and destructive white supremacy is. We see daily reports of violent harm done to those perceived as threats to those with power and privilege. Social media reports tally hundreds of thousands of human rights posts per day imploring the general population to question the bias that lives in each of us and take a stand for justice. Wariness of darkness has deep roots, and it is up to us to reorganize how we think about what we find threatening and why.

While we stare down a well of childhood fears, shames, and insecurities, many people are suffering now: children, marginalized populations, and immigrants.

Healing is power, and having power is having a voice. Having a voice means taking responsibility. We are far enough evolved to be able to address the destruction that is still unfolding. When we can bring what is nonconscious up to the surface for review, even more strides will be possible.

THE RETURN OF VITALITY

Making repairs with our inner child brings about healing and vitality. While the path is full of complexities, healing is a patient process and prioritized time is needed. Healing uses resources. When we begin to genuinely interact with our shadow, we can sense that every wound contains medicine.

Unhealed, we withdraw and withhold, confuse and create chaos. When we can acknowledge how we equipped ourselves for survival, we discover the treasure in healing. We begin to detect available energy to create an atmosphere for wellness for more than just ourselves. We are apt to let go of the excess we no longer need for false security, able to offer what we have to spare to ease another's way. When we develop a taste for loving what we thought was unlovable, generosity becomes a reflex and a value. This is the kind of "more" that is needed.

Adults with a wounded inner child have a special gift for helping other wounded children. It does not have to be your vocation, nor does giving back have to come in monetary form. In fact, money donations alone can be a way of bypassing what is really needed: attention, care, listening, dialogue, and action. Monetary generosity isn't going to cure the wounds being perpetuated in the greater community, though there are times when it is the key resource. With critical clues about what helps us, energy begins to stir and circulate. We awaken beyond self-centeredness and do not need all of the answers before helping others.

RELATIONSHIP IMPROVEMENTS

One of the most tangible rewards of unearthing your shadows and bringing them up to consciousness is the impact on your close relationships. Before I was aware of what my shadow was, my relationships were easily threatened by the conditions we were growing in. My peers and I did not have the skills to resolve hurts between us. Sometimes that meant holding onto resentments, only superficially moving on.

My later friendships were forged in soul work, and smack in the middle of triggering events: I had a second-term miscarriage, which caused my lifetime of ungrieved wounds to gape wide open, my mom got sober after decades of alcoholism and drama, and my depressed husband wasn't sure he wanted to be married after just three years. One of my friends got thyroid cancer, one lost her father, and another suffered an unrelenting loneliness. Yet another entered the divorce process after twenty-five years of marriage. We were all spiraling out in the bogs at about the same time. We moved through ten years of changes while sitting in a processing circle together to become aware of the spiritual illnesses resulting from our lived experiences.

Soul work flourishes in safe company that doesn't suffocate loved ones with shadow demands. Relief appears at every turn. Every healed part of the shadow-self welcomes in the sweetness of knowing that comes from surviving the hard truths. As I write, many around me are calling the shadows up from where they've been imprisoned and integrating them. I continue to drag the lake of the past as needed. Like the transformative process of soul retrieval, the forgotten, dissociated pieces of our past return to form more of the whole. This helps us show up to relationship more honest and more willing to be present to the needs of our close relatives and greater community.

REPARATIONS

Shadow work makes it possible to tune into matters that need all hearts on deck. If you are white or white-passing, heterosexual, and cis-gendered, you were born with assumed privileges. It needs to be understood that people without those privileges suffer in a system that does not prioritize or recognize an increased need for resources and protection.

Addiction recovery communities use a gesture called "lifetime amends." It represents an acknowledgment that the harm and the impact of the dysfunction caused by addiction is so far-reaching that only ongoing amends will build trust to heal. We are addicted to the benefits provided by our unearned privileges, and this harms many. Doing shadow work makes acknowledging and understanding privilege restorative, not exhausting.

It is redemptive to be devotional to the truth of oppressed and marginalized peoples, victims of genocide, and their descendants. Seek to understand ancestral and collective trauma. Center black, brown, indigenous, and queer people. Take an inventory of your reliable access to housing, healthcare, childcare, safety, security, education, retirement funds, creativity, and a job. Read statistics on gender and racial disparity. Make necessary amends to your immediate family members to practice awareness. Admitting error shouldn't raise your defenses.

Shadows cannot thrive where repairs are being made. Repairs soothe inflammation caused by previous generations' neglects. Making repairs can be the new norm when we are not offended by the needs and rights of others.

ME AND WE

The Western world is slow to value community as much as individualism. Time is calling us to develop skills for coping with individual pain so we are better equipped to address the systemic suffering that affects communities living with oppression.

The medicine in our wounds is to know them well, and with that wisdom, take responsibility for how our lives, *everyone's lives*, are turning out. When we take a higher level of personal accountability, we have the energy to fuel larger-scale reparative efforts. The wounds will still be there; they just won't be getting in the way as much.

While in your healing process, it is challenging to focus on others as much as yourself. It is a sacred time to devote to your wellness. The gold unearthed is found in clearing the path back to your soul's blueprint and living from it.

In order to take this work forward, you will need to believe that every soul is sacred and has a beneficial purpose. Evolution is showing us that in comparison to past generations, we are exceptionally open to new ways of being. We want more for ourselves, for the children, and for humanity from governing bodies and nations. Our cultivated desire for more has been provisioned by possessions, square footage, prestige, pseudo-comforts, and convenience. Our egoic desire for false forms of validation is shedding.

Shadow work is an inside job first, but its potential is to change the trajectory for all souls everywhere. It makes you safer within, and it makes the world a safer place.

BRIGHTENING

Embracing your shadow and calling out the collective shadows, and your part in reinforcing them, is empowering. It brings completion to the "Don't trust, don't feel, don't talk" ethics discussed by adult children of alcoholics (ACA) and addicts. Deep personal work sends us down into the basement of our being to confront the forgotten memories and dust off shelved emotions.

Investing in your soul work means creating a clearer future based on what is, rather than what we must fight to avoid. Opportunity and growth come from softening toward yourself and examining untruths. By divesting from false myths about yourself, you're moving away from denial and victimhood to become a sovereign director of your life.

There is sanctuary to be found in the dimly-lit hollows, even amid recollections of hardship. At the bottom of you is a you that was born valuable. Whether you were valued or not doesn't change that. This journey begins and ends with your willingness to participate in self-discovery. What you find will reveal the areas in which you will need more support.

You may determine that you want to create a habit of visiting your interior cavern to reconnect with what you know to be true about you. You may want to make amends to those you had shadow interactions with. You may want to cherish the part of you that adapted for survival with a celebration or ceremony. You may want to prepare for death in a sacred way. You may want to study historical accounts of liberation. You may feel increasingly able to express your liberation in a variety of ways: through art, writing, movement, language, singing, caring for those in need, and supporting people who need healing souls like yours to stand together with them.

What you do with your treasure is entirely up to you.

AFTERWORD

I'm imagining that there were parts of this book that may have been difficult to interface with. It's a big ask to invite you to volunteer your time and energy to becoming more whole through shadow work. I want to be transparent about my motivations for writing this book.

My own journey into the shadow realms first caused me concern. I did not yet understand how my distasteful, rejected parts could be of value to myself or anyone else. I only saw them as I did when the events were unfolding, by reliving the trauma. This led to anger for those who victimized me, and those who weren't present to protect me. The gifts of the shadow are not always apparent at face value. The shift came when I positioned my conscious self as a parent and the contents of my shadow as the lost children. My job was to reparent them with the empathy and compassion that was needed long ago. No one was going to be able to love their neglected appearances more than me. It was an inside job.

When we grow up without a reliable source of empathy, it's challenging to tolerate our shortcomings. On a difficult day, we self-abuse with internalized talk made of shame and criticism, perpetuating lies of unworthiness and lack. When dialoguing with the shadow children inside of me, I found my empathy muscle, and I began to tone and strengthen it. It was not easy to give myself room to make mistakes or challenge beliefs about myself and others based on their behavior and choices. The gift in gathering up these forgotten children into my lap is that I stopped allowing them to cause pain for others. My mind conjures images of my shadow children running up and kicking someone in the shins who they feared would hurt them, throwing rocks and then running to hide. To live reparented for empathy is to stop kicking, throwing objects, and hiding out when a threat is perceived, and assessing before reacting with more skill. It interrupts self-punishment and thoughts of being born to fail.

I am asking you to own your shadow. What that means is I want us to agree that I don't want my shadow running around hurting you, knowingly or unknowingly. I want you to protect me from your shadow, too. We must stop letting our nonconscious wounds and shadows act out.

Try this: when we look at our shadow like our hungry, ill-mannered, neglected, bullying, mean, greedy, and/or entitled child, we can see that every one of us needs to take care of our own child. It's a serious responsibility. At home, it is NOT OKAY to allow our wounds to wound others. In greater community it is NOT OKAY to harm or continue wounding marginalized peoples because the system was set up by colonial forefathers who did not consider how their intentions for liberty would play out on those they needed to labor and die for their endeavors. It has not meant freedom for everyone, just freedom for those willing to play by perverse rules. The medicine of our wounds is in knowing them, owning them, and stopping them from hurting ourselves and others.

Awareness and care create repair. Sometimes it requires nurturing that unruly child to investigate what is far beneath the surface, hidden by generations of unearned privilege and trauma. It's just like parenting our own children. We do not raise them well when we let our shadows do the disciplining—when we show up preoccupied, violent, distracted, self-centered, avoidant, and self-medicating. We have an epidemic of abandoned children living inside of us, and it's causing a crisis of abandoned living children. The result is that we participate in a world fueled by nonconscious greed—an enormous hunger for what can never satisfy or nourish us.

We raise indecent, violent children when we are hurting inside, and this in turn hurts them and their futures. They already know life is not about this empty feast. We betray their intuitive knowing by hardwiring them for the illusion of freedom. We give them a faulty template for happiness and success, just like we were given. This kind of freedom is keeping us and them in debt, prison, healthcare crisis, emotional chains, and stunted development that impedes thriving relationships. A thorough inventory of our individual and collective shadows yields a different kind of freedom— one that thrives on the liberation of all people from harmful learned behavior.

If your belief system or your religion hurts others, examine the shadows of its origins and what motives informed its policies. Be honest about the impact it's having. If people are being hurt by your beliefs, or the organization you affiliate with is teaching its participants to hurt, judge, or turn a blind eye to injustice, question it. You have the option to divest from sanctioned injustice.

It is a long road to unwind the shadows, but it is our work to do. Normalizing the unwinding process presents options. My strongest wish is that we prioritize freedom and justice for all—our ability to love, belong, and for each one of us to be free.

Love, Pixie

LANGUAGE PROMPTS

When I'm triggered, I'm not able to _____.

_____ causes me to respond with _____.

I'm finding it impossible to respond in a healthy way when _____.

As I unearth the past, I feel stronger about _____.

I'm in my healing process.

I'm asking for patience as I drudge up some pain that has really been impacting us.

I want better for me AND you, and this work is making that possible.

I'm in a shadow right now.

I'm reliving some painful moments from the past and need some time to find a way to tell you about it.

I need space to cry and rage about what still hurts.

I'm taking more responsibility for what I bring to our relationship.

This might get a little bit intense before things become clear.

I'm taking inventory of my sufferings in order to be more accountable for my reactions.

I'm sorry for how I came across.

What's really eating at me is _____.

I'm struggling with some old trauma.

I want to be a part of repairing the culture. This is my way of starting.

While I'm still lashing out in pain, we will continue to struggle.

I don't know what to do with what's coming up yet. You'll be the first to know.

My healing work will help bring my life into balance, and that serves us, too.

What's coming up for me is impacting the trajectory of my life and I'm determined to change it.

I may need to step away from our relationship for a little bit while I process what's underneath my strong reactions.

When I withdraw, it's because _____.

When I push you away, a very young part of me is wanting _____.

When I'm in fear, it limits me in these ways:

I'm incapacitated by my fear that _____ will happen.

I reenact the abandonment that happened when I was little to protect me from _____.

My biggest fear is that you will _____.

My biggest fear is that I will _____.

Sorting through the past will help me re-imagine my future.

I'm unwilling to allow my/your shadows to inform our relationship.

How can we support each other?

I don't want to dance with your shadow.

It is exhausting to be living in this loop.

I feel powerless in this moment, but with _____ I'll be able to get grounded.

I need to seek aggressive therapy for _____.

It re-injures me when I hear _____.

It really helps me to hear _____.

Let's have a productive talk when we are resolution-oriented.

It's taken me all these years to actually feel _____.

It's a relief to know that I don't have to _____ anymore.

Part of me feels _____.

I am getting to know myself in a new way.

There are parts of me I haven't allowed myself to show.

What's in my heart to share with you is _____. I want to feel safe to do that.

I'm taking ownership of my part in this breakdown by acknowledging that _____.

My part in my unwellness is due to _____. I'm doing _____ to change it.

When you're in a shadow, it helps me understand when you say _____.

Who I most need to share my pain with is _____.

I'm still feeling ashamed of _____.

I want to transform the persistent feeling of _____ inside.

In honor of transparency, I need to tell you _____.

I need some time to be with myself.

I'll check in with you when I get to the other side of this.

The time in my life that impacted me the most was _____.

I'm still suffering the loss of _____.

If I could go back in time and nurture myself through any hard time, it would be _____.

What I want is intimacy and closeness. Can we pencil in some time for that?

The reason I have such strong feelings about _____ is because _____.

The hurt part of myself wants you to know _____.

What does the hurting part of you like me to know?

Being this close to my pain makes me feel _____.

When I seem angry, I'm actually _____. (anxious, fearful, needing control, seeking reassurance, etc.)

When I shut down, it's because the child in me feels _____.

What I need most right now is _____.

I need to give consent on these matters: _____.

I need to have the freedom to _____. Is that possible?

My healing will take some time.

I hurt _____ when my wounds are in charge.

An amends that I would really like to make is _____.

If I could change some things, I'd start with _____.

When my shadow activates, I'm liable to _____.

I was asked to adjust for _____ when I was young.

I compromising my values in service to my woundedness in this area of my life:

_____ is suffering because of my unhealed wounds.

_____ helps me express pain in a way that gets my needs met.

My family suffered _____, and we are still feeling it.

_____ is my signature way of acting out my pain.

ACKNOWLEDGMENTS

Thank you to my friends and family, who held me up while this book claimed the spare space in my life.

Thank you to my children, who have received an early education on what happens when we stuff emotions.

Thank you to my unconventional partner, Sky Sharp, for co-creating a life that works for both of us.

Thank you to my dad for making it safe to share my messy feelings about our family shadows.

Thank you to Christena Cleveland for your dynamic support and points of view.

Thank you to Shannon Thompson for believing in this work and personal support.

Thank you to Joanna Price, Heather Dakota, and Henry Cordes, who helped me make this book beautiful, readable, and possible to be in your hands today.

Cherie Dawn Carr is the author of five books centered on healing through intimate relationship with oneself and the natural world. She is an enrolled member of the Choctaw Nation of Oklahoma. She writes as Lighthorse to honor the unheard voices of her ancestors.

Other Titles by Pixie Lighthorse

Boundaries & Protection

Prayers of Honoring

Prayers of Honoring Voice

Prayers of Honoring Grief